monospace

La Presse

PROVIDENCE & PARIS

2015

monospace
anne parian
translated by
emma ramadan

Monospace by Anne Parian

Copyright © 2007 P.O.L éditeur

Translation Copyright © 2015 Emma Ramadan

All rights reserved

Published in the United States by La Presse

an imprint of Fence Books

La Presse/Fence Books are distributed by Consortium

www.cbsd.com

www.lapressepoetry.com

Parian, Anne

Translated from French by Emma Ramadan

Monospace/Anne Parian

p.   cm.

ISBN 978-0-9864373-1-1

1. French Poetry. 2. Poetry. 3. Contemporary translation.

First Edition

10 9 8 7 6 5 4 3 2 1

We warmly thank the publisher of the original French edition of this book,
P.O.L Éditeur, for allowing us to publish this translation. You can see the
complete range of their marvelous books at www.pol-editeur.fr

a lovely tableau
a dining room
a birdhouse
a room for relaxing
a corner of shadow
a corner for wild animals
a bike garage
a tool shed
a band of sand on the sea
a covered path
a colonnade
an alcove
a stone bridge
a flight of stairs
a cedar's shadow
a bathroom
a cavern
an outhouse
a stream
a clothesline
an oil tank
a cutlery drawer
a black marble clock
a big bouquet
a plaster cupid
an avenue of poplars

laid out as obstacles
and certain insurmountable
cuts

no rush
used to detours
all that can be
is kept

the box of Petits Lu
the ceramic sink
the gas water heater
the bush in the path
the cool fountains
the mossy pass
the geography book
the cardboard assemblage
the decorated chair
the metal desk
the stone bench
the high windows
the broom closet
the big lawn
the niche in the hedge
the campfire
the rock collection
the little boat and the little lake
the beaten field
the view from the balcony
the uneven trail
the tap water
the verdant pasture
the greenhouse oasis
the outskirts of the park
the flimsy drape

beyond compare

without sorting without restoring

The Scenery

Knowing nothing about flora the large and small vegetation is represented by color or contour[1]

Leave the arrangements of a few shared places to their number[2]

One unhappy hour the garden breaks away from the image of such irrefutable diligence naming new patterns at its discretion

A display in the smallest possible space of the smallest common factor of an undefined but stable state corrected by sentiments of possible praise or a realized impulse

1. Fix the scene on a map. To the south, the warmth-seeking plants, a decorative heap of vines with black fruit in the first row, covered in catuflorus and rampant ceanothus. All thwarting harmony.
2. Am I unaware of what fantasy, of what the picturesque, can do for the tired spirits seeking variety as a cure for their weariness?

Inevitably there remains something antique used to reproach both the rustic and the obstinate in certain folds even if they can't be justified

yes

Captive eyes everywhere spectacular realizations the view gets lost from now on quietly out of sight[3]

Motion and sound subject to wind temperature and light create remarkably predictable sparklings held in a little frame[4]

3. This time it's not a matter of position: the illusion of retreat dissolves, even though I mention it again.
4. The sun itself veiled by dark clouds and fake rain whenever I want.

The drawing is composed of objects pools clearings breezes shelters the invention of space as if created in your wake a place for you to settle[5]

But what's it all about?

Doing it daily methodically no pattern could convince anyone that the chosen features[6] are the most necessary however much they are fed by habit and cliché

How else?

5. That's what I'm looking for.
I arrange the models according to my whims.
6. I don't regret the various tints or the pale gnomes, lively, fluorescent, even if they discredit the whole and force us to begin again. I must not give in.

Changes in the air beyond our expectations cutting bit by bit through
this discovery

I don't know anything about it
Each addition perfects the perceptible whole

Promontories placed to give rise to forms ways and overall views
allowing repetition by mass and by sequence
overall view
exchanged in an instant[7]

---

7.   So watch as I repeat myself and never stop considering the minor details. I keep track of
the rumors and each thing thought. I imagine the opposite all the time. The smallest doubt
dispenses with sense and my reply.

Start out tracing lines from the farthest point of view[8] while you always calmly always slowly drift away on chaotic paths breathing easy

The traditional rhythmic metaphoric quick figurative pace is obvious[9] pursue it or for no reason stay[10]

8. Following the view
to the infinite vague horizon
sway the dry pathway plastered with maples
bordered by tratiacus by swamp silt
9. That I don't know how to keep it together doesn't ruin the rest.
A real pleasure in the face of difficulty, when the very desire for preservation impedes all progress.
10. In a despite-myself manner
undeniably ideal
I want to invent everything myself
and yet no

in the tension hold yourself
in the tension bursting

Call it *Monospace*[11]

Ready for a new day on a new terrain of shapes where many of these
fading things will slowly finish up

Just a thought between the condensed interior and the enlarged
exterior
the scenery[12]
how to find yourself no matter what[13]
landscape[14]

11. So poorly am I able to create a new internal order, vehicle, terrain, guinea pig formations,
I plan the whole to be quite simple and its elements as obvious as possible. Yes, but what's it all
about?
12. You see that after all I'm only interested in the world we live in, so why would I preserve
the rest as scenery?
13. The neatly classified pages of notes and plans are of no help at all, though at times they
are a great comfort.
14. I put everything in its exact though temporary place on the map: avenues, lawns,
plantings, ponds, walls, follies, buildings, entryways, plains, prairies, forests, snow, bridges,
carousels, boats, oceans, rivers, highways, etc.
A shield of trees and parallel planks encloses the ornamental result and forms a jarring,
charming basis whose plans I overplay.

For example the great middle path of land in raw sienna

When all is said and done the task is to use the available surface well[15] carefully-drawn plans for a garden, for example, don't just suddenly happen[16]

imagine you are the most skillful builder of the most novel spaces

no one should be chained to less noble work

15. Even though the maps minimize elevations and developments in their definitive forms.
16. All gardens have their oddities, some follies, pagodas, aqueducts, hermit's huts. And their function, to give flight to fantasy, must be taken seriously by the range of opinions, as volatile as possible, graceful, benevolent, astonishing.

The terrain is framed by lines two horizontal and two vertical
which give rise to a number of verticals and horizontals unlimited
interpolated[17]

The overall look planned as an autonomous whole in an abstract
space is the same when at the same places changes seem different to
the eye and to the foot[18]

17. I assign squares an axiomatic value. From one to the other, all sorts of passages: tortuous,
fluid, convenient, sumptuous, obstructed, or loud. Or perfect.
18. Because I arrange it all during my walks, I usually go back to the same places and try to
pause; it's the best way to get some perspective and to deepen my observations.

Pose in front of this cube or that line
measure the ridge a little farther down
cut out now

The names of sienna cobalt tyrien venetian focus the difficulty[19]

Better
the yellow angle in the oak undergrowth riots thickets summits

Half of the time the project finally revives white by default drawing
these conclusions together

19. Finding the material surprisingly satisfying, I don't worry about the mixing of mud and
color.

I dig out and extend the streams on maps
to remain in the breeze and astonishment
of aquatic fauna
of dragonflies and marshes
and to preserve this damp dark corner
of mosquitoes
contrasted
and corrected

At the same time make a global representation
a burrow
and inside it put the collection of colored boxes so that the seasonal
changes[20] safely circulate between them

Wood piles and cardboard[21] demarcate the zone enclosing a small
mobile object position unknown compared to a bigger more stable
object position known

20. Seduced by ideas of wanderings and almost-hidden narrow passages, I lose myself.
21. Here I place a lot of little objects: clocks, lamps, vases, garlands, statues, showing off their
uselessness.

The model brought back to two dimensions[22] following stretches
either gray or colored[23] to open onto breathtaking panoramas[24]
that call into question any hint of profundity
stars depths seas
fears and habits concealed[25]

Quiet and forcibly unnoticed inclination in the twilight friendly forest
of morning dreams

22. I try to divert attention away from the vanishing point, but it's conspicuous from
everywhere and disrupts each near view. Panoptic irrelevance when it comes to motion.
23. I stop using oranges and reds two seasons out of four, which, like the lilac, are dreary
when not in bloom.
24. Every time the same practical decisions
lift this loose slope
consider each layout reversible
destabilize in small fractions
25. I keep myself in a felted shell
smiling smooth blissful fish

An illusion to start from

animals to hunt
reunited for now

the low volume flows down the slope as if on a slipping wooden floor
and the level doesn't matter the overall effect swells and persists in an
unavoidable grid and there
take that path

run away

crossing of little bridges[26] over the waiting obstacles of a troubling
prefabricated pattern[27]

26. I was going to jump the barrier
but not jumping is fine a bleating
sheep
before the look strays
to the mundane countryside
27. Collection of cheap trash
filled with references as distant as they are exact
I realize the problem a few pages later

The unique use of frankly unstable seated postures[28]

Believing it's possible to balance

Chairs attitudes epochs all fixed we recognize ourselves in them[29]

Decorative foliage and hybrid animals traced on red marvels armors and staffs[30]

Medicinal plants chosen for their aesthetic value or medicinal virtue

28. I prefer folding chairs
to rest or reflect
they perk me up
though they mock me with their garish colors
29. Deliberate strip, bodies borrowed from diverse and precise lessons from the Far East.
From them I learn, little by little, the nuances, the pleasure.
30. Labeling epochs and goals remains decisive. When I'm not bothered by the overall unity,
design yes, order no.

Finding good lighting for each setting isn't easy[31]

A few temporary lights allow a trace of low intensity illumination
from one line or the other of trees of a farm or prairies bordered by
trenches

Tricks of sudden brilliant bursts
rushing describing
a grid of decisive gain for the maximum effect

A mute majestic animal courtyard the figure of an elephant instinctive
habits and arabesque grace of unmoving objects[32]

Ambition slides over to the improved decorations
discontinued

31. I move mythical form
some candles in hand
my trivial form exposed
32. I look out,
ghostly at the window

Open views ease the long waits at the threshold[33] and allow descents
crossings wanderings as if slowly affirming synthetic plants and their
dispositions in the cross-outs
or defaults

The observer must wait a while for the view to change[34]

33. I decorate the most distant points: a tree, a statue, a bench, a pond, a bed of rocks, a bed of
roses, a small island of isolation.
34. You can you lean like me there
under the pressure of changing winds

The shaky heap is a hell in disorder[35]

Refined in the noisy pine
fallen from branches the cicadas take up their scrapings

All is well

Not just any type of vegetation
Those wanting in green
are garbage[36]

That's right

---

35. Parallel lines connect objects of different planes. The line of this column cuts the line of
that row which I then show off in a clearing.
36. The dynamics of color work according to the most common use of some sort of vague
language.

The open circular space reserved for spare moments[37] is planted with
trees and cleared anew

Like a point from above ideally small ideally round that can take
infinite shapes in its earthly form

Dotted lines and small serrations join in the unlimited field
of points

Dissemination of landmarks
rendered on postcards
remember reverse reflect[38]

37. Where we break from all discomfort.
Decisions to make within disorder.
38. While you listen to me there is a double meaning that refuses balance

The surrounding wall fortifies the lively insides of figurines
determining possibilities for stretching
the stories

Consequences of random events named by families of actors[39] of
objects of intentions
no matter

Vague recollections

39. My intentions for those absent are neutral.

The slowing speed sadly does not prevent questions about rules and
systems about manners and forms
the tools[40]

Each addition perfects the whole

40. When certain tools resist fatigue, they seem to possess an impossible power.

The quality of the tools testifies to the temptation to disrupt the whole for a taste of imperfect
use

as I sometimes imply
and you still deny
with conviction
why?

The arrangement of frames on the layout divides the space in a fluid geometry that follows the footprints of wanderers sometimes outlined in their driftings[41]

it's the same

without the distress of a scene described in its dingy yellow less special tones

At last build a tent from piles and planks with rows and poles that slice the designs[42] and keep the curious at bay

41. Followed to the rose garden despite myself
where I thought I'd see you.
42. Time stolen, I keep figures at a distance, witnesses in the stands.
The circle of friends extended
a conglomeration of faces of smiling princes
and princesses leaning over balconies.

I sense your distraction
but you're not here
for no reason.

The photographs from near and far show the model the masses the colors from every angle[43] and
help decide which parts to hide

Curtain

Adopting a dominant point of view lets you get closer to the underlying idea

The general outline traced with the help of pickets has perhaps disappeared

---

43. The most objective form of a map, as I mentioned before, is the grid. The most objectively calm, it produces a fatal cold, and it's no accident that I use it more and more.

Luminosity density the greenery that sparkles

Climbers insects birds fill the foliage proffered to the most majestic predators[44]

say it

Exotic moss stones sand and snow preserved under powerful spotlights[45]

44. A zoo inspired at every turn by savage nature irregular lines wind under the unchecked effect of the elements.
45. Like you, I'm satisfied with lines supplied to me by commerce

The colored boxes multiplied in series for parties and useless
creations
Shaped magic adapted to anything
only
under good conditions

Certain painters offer models for walls pillars rocks waterfalls fields
and ruins skies barriers doors and caves[46]

and it only takes three or four years for a patina to appear on recycled
materials[47]

---

46. You see that I duplicate them to understand something, to do something that you, like me,
still don't know how to do.
47. For building partitions, I prefer compact materials that block out all sound. No one should
be disturbed by noises or words addressed to another; at the same time, no one should be
forced to whisper.

Using familiar furniture allows different organizations alignments
series accumulations
not linked to plantation not linked to circulation

geometries or pyramids of plastic tables and chairs
green or white

whose abundance increases the hesitation the gradual cessation
obstinate joy disorder
and dissemination[48]

48. Abandoning old habits, you were sleeping, in the dark, so close, fresh and delicate, at my
side.

Break away from formal ideals[49]
the minimal models pique interest less decoration[50]
however refined or erudite[51]

Recognize their uselessness

Monochrome of dominating blues

it sleeps our critical capacity

sleeps

49. A distinct view of the circumference, for example, of a muddied puddle, lost in the background, and maintained that way.
50. Galvanized wire is held on the walls horizontally by hooks, the most costly support for climbing plants.
51. For example, worn old planks and low-end plastics, highlighted with cheap gilding, angelic flights and floral clouds, little bouquets of violet, carmine, and canary, forming a modest unity from my moderate choice.

Useless detours along the bleak back walls of laborious buildings

narrownesses

on the lovely sullied maps the mud throughout blurs the ideal
lightness of lively inscriptions[52]

From the other side only
the vast fields
sprawling

52.   I know those walls left free for the scribbles drawings graffiti scrawlings of wanderers,
repainted white on the hour.

Specters multiplied inside leafy cradles divided and surrounded by
fences[53]

Extraordinary effect of geometric assemblages
more
interior transformations to the existing model even if not easy
on the eye

Art of the ways they say that act at their discretion[54]

Shapes tests and colors on a small scale allow a freer expression that
must be treated meticulously

whitewash

53. I cross out as much as possible, though it can be discouraging.
54. Overwhelming for the novice
but not too complicated
assemblages random specks
a limit to what I can say
to what you can say
say it
and don't do it
except under the cover
of new landmarks

Flat from identical delicate touches[55]

Nuances
Habits
Calculations

Gentle doubt about the adopted formula the method the emulation
the game the stripes[56]
with the learned impulse to handle transitions no friction
and the now final form that we demand every night with no
tomorrow

for example a Monday[57]

55. I fiddle with things.
The force of electrical, mechanical, synthetic machines changes and channels the voice, the
image, the movement, all under new forms.

A miracle (nervous)
a miracle nothing less
56. All movement blocked by an element
with which no relation is possible
the voices converging
from all sides encouraging
57. I like that this amounts to little effect and that you only vaguely remember it.

Keep a convex shape the expression of a unique interior space
astounding eternity
delight[58] of hidden havens behind
the screens which heed their construction

From a nearby angle fly to the opposite linked by twine in a single
line

arabesque[59]

58. I often return to the lack in the background, from all points hidden, developed for the
interim.
59. Here are the plants drawn and deployed in the air, replanted by specialists at the ideal
temperature.

Mental note
tighten the strings of the bouquets

pines
cicadas

Through each development, I perfect my methods
and mean to be taken inexhaustibly seriously.

A lovely situation ruined through continual collapse

Where can we go for fun
you say[60]

Rush of an underground pass breaking out onto a half-world
without faults

Butterflies

So many embroidered patterns insects alighting on tapestries
and don't question the tiny space that concentrates our attachment

A line of benches in a simple little path see some trees planted under
sheds

60. I describe piles and ruins
embellished with past uses
and fiddle with things
Domesticated dogs, cats, birds
held by so many ribbons and chains

Nothing justifies wandering
or not doing so

the usual monologue
opt halfway up for the panoramic half-map projected
with no hindrance or horizon

and run back to the museum[61] verify the colors lines and contours
meditative virtues of perfect views[62] without throwing yourself in and
abusing the sound with echoes

61. Once there, revise the available scales; pastoral proportions, movements of nudes, natures,
figures, models. As you know, I always go back.
62. I keep the colors, lines, and contours, their meditative virtues; I never have the patience
to stay.

I want to leave even the garden
because its tableau is enough.

We're not sure how long we can stay here

the question of heating
the irritation this half-dead plant its green
branches like a rose[63]

But stop going for walks at night

instead blend in with the shadows glide into the arms of a man or a
woman willing to do anything in order to sleep

Harmonious
flowing repetitions determined in the bliss of beautiful mornings

if not a preference
unconfessed
for solitude and silence

63. Emphasized in the overall vision that disrupts the proliferation of parasitic effects, kept
from lack of interest.

Fold up the map extend the curves stretch the color multiply the motifs purify the whites move the familiar figures into a room that looks out onto an orchard

Throw out

the objects in the foreground that don't work asparagus carafe shoes debris stuffed poultry[64]

It's not uncommon to get the wrong diagram or a base that doesn't take you anywhere except sometimes backwards[65]

64. A lot of sketches for one detail, and if I don't find certain long lost patterns it's best to create them anew, use them in place of the old forgotten ones, indifferent.
65. I have abandoned the original garden, and my method of describing it. Before returning to the project, say that you expected it from me, the complexity, piling on excitement, the joys of intertwining color.

Stoop down stand up stoop down stand up stop from time to time[66]
look up at the sky wipe your brow
What then?

At the instant of formal conviction a fundamental behavior with no
courtesy or consideration choose an arrangement in the smallest most
neutral corner[67] rich with the initial immensity
see
the kept cardboard edging

66. Pause in a closed hiding place
a green square secluded in all seasons from a view of the unruly countryside
67. I get somewhere where I can sit down get up sit down get up look at the sky

Wheelbarrow shovel and spade
tricks contradict and play
with paint
imminence without method

All the drawings applied precisely to the inner design balanced by a
wild virgin indivisible nature[68] allow the copies
to multiply the presentations of foliage of different scenes and varied
positions

---

68.   The jungle effect will be staged in scholarly terms: *phyllostachys aurea, pontic rhododenron, sedge, primulas, ligularias cotoneaster damneri, hereda helix* and *acaena,* for example, reinforced by the power of suggestion, maintained by the tap of the movements of reliefs, the synthetic materials, the plastic fabrics, the disposable paper.

The angles don't alter the pace of the changing circles lunar craters
and visions popping up right under your nose

The scenery takes form from the desire to describe it alone
so flat

the blue of its only side cloudy skies less and less believable mosaic
view

you watch it fall apart[69]

69. The ideal elevation remains, despite the sound of its crumbling.

Take care of the polished parts of the shallow ponds animated
with intermittent bubblings populated with luminescent and
interchangeable
fish
for all
droplets with spontaneous effects
bounce back
and sieve

Wash and polish
on a daily basis look after
the scratches in the paint[70]

---

70. I refuse to treat the polluted water or any other filth in order to emphasize the repulsive
nature of the most disgusting places.

An enchantment without thorns or sharp edges

Normally only possible to surprise on the flat side
To cushion softly is a favor

The ideal reliable territorial versions of an earlier place
isolated tiny they blur the choice of population
Baroque agreement among things that arrange themselves[71]

Some useless gates open close open close[72] hide narrow passages lit
by round neon greens that refresh the synthetic grass

71. In the moment I second-guess the layout of the room where we meet.
72. I have to assure myself of the closings, their repetition doesn't matter.
At best, their use in the site will have been forgotten.

On a small scale around a little bench

A blueprint details the technical models and the discoveries of
harmonies that don't spoil the peaceful views[73]
numerous effects ideally mundane matched to the simple style[74]

Comfort yourself with this emblematic idea:
let it be[75]

partitions hedges flowers
divide up the paths

and it's nothing but disorder

73. However, due to dubious temporary lighting, and constrained by an alternative overall
movement, I neglect the views for now.
74. Carried by the rhythm of the constant repetition of identical intervals, I walk straight
towards the vanishing point.
75. To this I am grateful for my newfound freedom.

The meticulous study of vegetation allows re-plantings and
alignments when it's for a common definition or a colored stain
it's precisely with that[76]
in a sudden certain way
take a gamble on a section of vertical strokes
when so many dark figures move
against the typical background of little animals

don't touch them

76. The treatment of surfaces according to their color
at the edges light wakes up moving
lights of dreams
on the mysterious and familiar apparitions
precise dates of assemblages
content with the new impressions

I lay down in the grass to think about some strange success, looking for the deepest shade.

The panel leaning against the porch for the first time the fence rolling
on a red façade contradict the paradisiacal moment posed as ideal
it's no secret

The house plants geraniums begonias whatever
at the windows
never noticed[77]

are the base of my installation

77. I hear you discuss my approach to all things, even trivial.
Even improvised, my indifference is refined, you say.
I wear myself out with the random materials
of post-dream mornings unfit for eloquence
to which I am drawn, despite myself
though that doesn't really worry me

I rise in my usual way roll towards the center[78]

and later I'll leave a display of mythical dwarf shrubs settled there
and on the ordinary wood of the threshold
my slippers[79]

truly

I begin again

78. This painting
when you find yourself there again
and something else
that I fearlessly strive to describe
when you're happily paying attention
I want to believe
and that may be

79. I mention their color
as a general characteristic

I begin again

80. I exaggerate the model's mimeticism; associations of uniform behaviors at the idea of success or of an effect whose sparkle is only known at a small scale.
81. It is also good to know that there are other ways of doing it, but why?
Search for something less archaic in my designs search.

I make a clean sweep

and advance in this garden where vegetal sounds swarm, as if conceived by a painter
82. Curl up in the sheets and covers give the methods a momentary limit whose consciousness I know how to prolong.
83. I'd have the hardest time convincing you to persevere, not neglecting any approximation, searching for the ideal nature, even to begin again indefinitely out of fear, refusing not to reach it.
84. I appreciate the hidden vices of procedures or materials
the deep water fish for
their inconceivable coordination in the shadows
and hope to know nothing of nature moved to the point
where a line crosses the map leaning fence
balance
fall
or chaos

of so many changes

I begin again

I Begin Again

I start over with stains that evade the moving colored shadows
I repeat

Monospace is clearly not original

a series of forced manipulations I track on a screen

Keep or erase

remember the mark of happy nature on naked bodies

its hypothesis

swimmers raised in modest
attitudes
still
undefined

A careful approach sketching the common effects
the reproduction is entirely vague
I remain vaguely on this side
the middle
supported I break away from this large line
litter of resounding gravel
on grass

Keeping track of my involuntary movements I work on a panel
decorated with pastoral patterns

objects
rocks
familiar fruits as good as the open countryside
rectangles borders grids look
stay
no margin no limit

I begin again

The seat the façade the green plot
sprawling mass
gray

eminent

No matter what limits I prescribe to night visions

a concern spreads
the bed made
delicate with some moss
synthetic glue
and future
in truth

finally

What would I have done without
exercise without patience for transitions
no collision

I was vague about the extent of possible discoveries

for no reason

After the fact I find a common kind of eclipse to keep myself focused

on a vision when it crosses
a more or less
impossible distance

Certain mixed circumstances distant views and pursuits carelessly
rush my commitments

Pursue this path look for precision in the many models
in order to believe it

I give the name compost
to each sprout in the pot
(times past)
obeying the material
called raw
and green

for now better to be convinced and follow
closely

a wish

future variations
no one says that they hinge
on a chance of success

First problem

a garden is never ideal

it resists the effects appearing without follow-through repeated with
joy

I begin again

the roots spreading out on each side I throw the whole so that it is
reflected
under the radar of perception

of interphenomena of drawings of stains
of style

I watch it like that lifted up mechanically like that whatever it is

a condensed image
look and see why
I might not have recognized it before

Note it for the end of July and forget it before planting Acanthus
Sea holly
Abelias

perfection corrected from now on
refined you say in new classic connections

that I try to emphasize

Whatever my fantasy
whatever the form I arrange flowers and castles
in a simple pattern
with some suspicion
beech and holly symmetrically
why

I highlight straight lines
up close a touch of gilding along a little field a seat equally ornate

confusion

some lines enclose the design some understand when to ask for a
solution

the least conceivable
on paper

enjambment

Vaguely executed maps and descriptions based on the designs leave
the theoretical field open

a garden

that I watch you walk across

such noise if it must be marked machinery

the tools that I approach with only the help of an encyclopedia send
me the photograph
the spade the rake the tractor
the automatic sprinkler
don't screech
images fixed depths moving voices
muffled
maps multiplied
mostly by season

Note the names of the flowers

the most tangible colored effects create more diversity than I know
how to show

They ask me what it is
My answer is odd because I'm not a gardener or an architect or an
historian

Hatchings in season and sprinklers in rows describe the stages where
my worry and curiosity change nothing

I'm no longer hoping

I go for a blend of states that those now or once good at entertaining
enact without any confusion of effects
rising to run
resting on benches

observe one's actions on the supposed other

a clear constructivist system
soon outdated I regretted why in real time can't I see the end

I begin again

and trace my creations in the dramatically altered familiar historical
styles of anecdotal memory sure of seriously succeeding

I move all the small stuff

the many objects I know how to put together in many ways in the
synthesis of the hypothesis

concerning the limits of liberty

You go rambling
through imitations confabulations simulacra to reach a dimension far
from perspective

making the vanishing point into an object
filing off in two directions

flashes and fortunes
unusual in their useful state

I spread out
and associate elements
and principles
not worrying about the ferocious figures that look like me

My creations are my ideals I describe the minute countryside
saturating it with everything

whitewash

I am its painter

I am not its painter

whitewash

up close
looks farther
look for shortcuts

I walk in a flat dimension something soft under foot and pliant lines
intersecting beneath my steps

elementary

I arrange space and scenery arbitrarily giving no reason for my choices

I start again with the painting
Bonnard ideal not for the brushstroke or the light but for the foliage
white black like that
undercover
I propose the regretted pose of different old experiments though not
in any photograph

Erase

and colors and contrast improve
and despite everything in the archaic way framed by a grid I meet the
challenge of a general diagonal opening out

I seize every opportunity for the sweeping strokes of monochrome
motifs

An instant without the rhythm
of blinking lights
the inextricable conjunction of little details
I multiply the knots

What can I do?

Detach from the decorations those effects that are general visual and
traditionally unusual

around a fountain the flowered lawn
surrounded by bushes hills groves
all green

There's no real ridgeline without the ruins of what I'm trying to do
for example change the scale to make larger drawings possible

Ovations

I show the stars look to my son
who watches all of them alone

I called a small enclosed space ideal world like others removed as far
from thought as possible as sober as available

A small space deserted by fault of having been drawn without a hitch
in its reflexive variety closer to that faith without the astonished
model

I reveal and resolve as if someone with more experience than I
wouldn't make the same mistake

or worse

nothing else
can be considered that's all I want

here it is

trust this model made by my hands according to my idea
picturesque also calm
shadowed
distinct from all that's drawn

I have other objectives rather better however
you refuse them if I stop

stop then go on

To cross or repeat for example shows me a shady drawing nearly
arrested nevertheless right where I look for what I'm looking for
foreign
inscribed in an equal square
fear form fixed sketched
from systems of new facts that I know how to end correctly skillfully
by habit of

yellow sun
pale moon
finite sky

so that we have under our eyes
a still indivisible mass

I apply myself to gardening with method
patience and precision
I use the simplest practice arrange matching plants in regular rows of
decreasing length
blues
yellows
greens
which bloom in turn

The sparse with the simple promises a lot but why
I don't deny
give it limits
economic expression
clear
wouldn't you say

Monospace is conversely luxurious accused of using indecisive details I
describe its unbalanced arrangements alphabetically

abelia wallpaper does not give
names of flowers only an idea
in this instant
of the potential
for the infinite
reproduction of Abelias
pretending perspective

There's a form that takes up the principle so I give in to its evidence
although reluctant

I assumed it had an excellent position for unstable observation
suspended in the foreground

orthogonal lines and
flights
seasons
stacks of stumps

I understand that like an outdated system
it brings about real doubt

you'll be able to say how
I didn't believe it

make it happen or let it happen

categorize
when I begin again
surprises
desire to be above all
surprising

my role in the whole
lights on the fences guide wanderers with dazzles

uncontrolled

Repetitions

Go off often without looking
or staying
would I look for it
now that I don't believe it
by collecting comforts
without sufficient aid or ways
unstable
without the support
of that which we
carelessly remember

The gargoyles up high on the marquees watch the fountain in the center
the entered space
with no drawn trajectory

I criticize the flight the momentum the rush
the jostled crowd
wants to detach itself from conventional conditions

applause

The eye traces a line
because it is better
for it to stay broken
acutely angled

Angles sharp and active
polychrome inside

Despite myself I add to
this hybrid artifice

sharpness
of a diagonal line
of an identified flight
in the known route
the night turns
sharply dark

I push my momentum to extreme
limits

You will say that I don't know the risks of such heavy equilibrium
that I don't know
this system's blurred approach
or the grid without elevation

Tributary to the observer's
impressions tired
of the old method savoir-faire
complicated at random

substitutions
reports
inversions
divides

I put the finishing touches on the project tight points against lines in
white blocks

farther down
perfumed

completed by
statues and clocks

Always refining something unfinished and no one can ask why I do
what I do

seriously
everything's fine

I brag
about choosing
from dispersed and
amalgamated things
the granite the flat rocks mounted
in an equilateral triangle

against the flat sky that envelops it
the roof of tiles on slate
looks strange

On a map of shallow waters
for example enclosures
adorn a thorny hedge
I add the metal trellis
at regular intervals

taciturn and pictorial
habits

I choose to lose the density
replace one work with another
complete and delineate the ensembles
which illuminate a theory

which is this

a familiar adaptation
its ordinary use
attests a twisting of taste
so close
in the small space
where my project takes place
I simultaneously evoke
many contrasting pieces
for which I don't have
a solution
in isolation

Beyond the margin
I make a dock out of planks
and jump to the other side

assuming you followed me
diagonally

There you can't care about the figures
the motherly woman placed
in the foreground
smaller in the background
growing distant in the sunset

I try to reveal which precise place
gilt-edged
witnessed my birth

would be a momentary memory
you see perfectly
that I speak with you about it
as I do with the others

I arrange
rows of wood
ties of twigs
and rotting leaves
mixed with tar
without sacrificing anything to the volume
or weight of each

It's fire

I want to replant
to rake over a large part
to extend
to make circles

I'm still raking

turning away from pots aligned
advantageously on the columns
seen from below unchanged
by excess lighting
by brightness
emphasized pointlessly
in the first place

I strain myself a little over the drawings
affect the allure of strict concentration

fixed

on a complex phrase
an eminent event
I will let loose the layout of a new observation
in a rigidly enclosed order

neon gated cubes

with no principal point of view
or mastery of effects dispersed
on clouds

shown to my son

Foresee all
that the unknown requires
of the flexibility
that I feign
of a discordant and rapid
touch that exceeds the whole
each sampled tone
from this to that to the point of saturation
a coat of green

I substitute
a sprawling
and repetitive vision
for the conclusion

I lead you understand
all at the same time refolded
incompatible
and tactless

yes tactless

you see

I use
what lasts

I give my idea
a slightly silly form and you take it
easily
even though it combines
all kinds of material
in uncertain
and even contradictory
conditions

Other half-world

Half-basin of open air

of the lethal effect at the moment it appears
in this playroom
I isolate some isoclinic
shadows

shattered

don't think there's no time for the small objects I've always thought
about
preferring shortcuts
unadorned

From a prominent perspective
of an ideal situation
I don't see a thing
yet persist in this daily excess and exaggerate the effects
blindly disordered

The melancholy
isolated from initial nomadic
maps

The sacred beasts come out of ditches
continuing the detritus

That's all

Mondrian's earthy period
the varnishes the
begonias

beneath a list of botched apparitions
the chirping of cicadas in the passage
the hypothesis of a classic polychrome field
on chipboard

Despite the mediocrity of the means and materials I acquire
some designs that match my whims
rest
and fantasies
of overused virtues

and that's not all

An alignment of sculptures
stuck at an angle to the ground

cements
partitions

beyond dreams until now
only silent intentions

in the certainty of rebuilding
without insisting

The edifice finished for a laugh
and with what draw which
other perspective
advanced by guesswork
all the notations
of stable elements
in disorder

all the porticos

a risk at the level where you sleep

and you'll conclude
won't you
with a gesture
sharp from so far away
and vague

Cézanne or Rubens
similarly named Paul

I seriously imagine something
which holds this or that
together
and serves us

I match one thing with
the other clashing so that
you'll see the effects
in reverse

arranged at every
resemblance
satisfied
in a dimension that I
repeat to see
I repeat
that it's not going anywhere

according to what idea

I lean
over the fluorescent
lizard
leave me
if I move
quick

leave

Gradually I guarantee
a system of camouflage
from one point to the other
formless

vast supple surfaces
where it sinks
into the idea of erasure
of familiar stature
whose crude manner ensures
an original confrontation
with a view to new examples

You see the mobile
frames
less and less the photographs
an exposition where time is
the condition I tell you
now

stop

no hesitation
no evocation
don't agree on the singular qualities of shadow
or heat

I redefine the dominant
yellow sketch
of a perfect line

You wouldn't expect moderation in my contradictions
why would I avoid the volatile materials

whitewash

permanent
yes

extension of dimensions arms legs of a person of average size

I keep this green this orange
one drips without the other
and the azaleas get better

The quirks of my meditation hold on to the probable expanse to the
variety of possible
behaviors

Retouching the photographs
I address each aspect
each tone
exactly
I don't neglect any part of the layout
of these enchantments

it's a waste

whatever the moment
the routes needed
to maintain the circulation
of shelter of furniture
of often unequal happiness

you see me without resources

I express myself poorly re the difficulty you know it recurrent that
opposes proportion with certain lines of half-mastered formulas

enjambment
constraints

that I choose myself or stop myself
observed for instance
in a sustained pose
I believe

I doubt the position
of the observer weak from magnified
visions

I don't worry

about the idea of a result
pushed back
as far as possible
to a fragile construction that assumes new expression and sometimes
won't be mistaken
except for a forsaken rule

The small stuff never served for lack of adapted traditional know-how

don't deny it

Each arrangement escapes
how
seedlings sprinklers
frames ruins squares
how
treats the demonstration of its exemplary necessity
why

classes of species escape
burdens twitches
deceits

past mimicking profundity
preferable
to then name everything differently

present the views the designs in the biggest grids

I outline this possibility
for you too

I especially remember the bathers barely conscious of the visitor
walking away

I stand more
soberly on the threshold
at the moment important
for coming back to you

freely

More precisely the motif of gathering ruins
congeals the memory in a frieze at the bottom of the wall

It's clearly ideal to get rid of all that and just follow a path
fix your gaze in the distance
well above
beyond or

close your eyes

A final touch before letting go of this project whatever the execution
however

it's tangled

Obliged to oversee inspiring possibilities I fix the brakes or the speed
its surplus
escapes

The missing details allow a constant variety that could even without
order maintain anyone
removed even
removed
in this obsessive concentration summoning an heroic ideal you see me
use the fixed figures unequally

I lean towards you
outside my designs
keep sleeping you like
the night just as well
a room
skewed projection
of a simple place

Curtain

I brighten the colors of the closest
mountains
herbariums
red and white points
path of yellow grass falls
water into water
and stained with these black
gnats in little waves
I erase the name

There's nowhere else to stray you say

Curtain

Inventory of little locales I try to describe
the beginning of their beautiful formation

Hurry

no matter hope
I can
somewhat rushed manner
to confuse
the dream has to end

hope

again for a laugh
isn't it
applause

linked with the initial idea of the garden theater of love I can't get
back to the moment
seasons nor castles

Made only of grass
or only of trees
formations of islands and adventures
possible from the first song
the whole
confirms the unity required
for an exhaustive
composition

Seed of a new paradise

Wind of the east against the wearying south
antique masses
assaults of forces
that break the orthogonal

a point

Slabs lifted up in the sun to uncover a meadow nearby
fragrant though full of animals
enemy
familiar
lambs and lions

Sit down here

You sit down here
gold finches canaries
I sit down here
partridges nightingales
blackbirds conks linnets
singing reverberated
against the child's anxiety
that no one survives faced
with too many monsters

Silhouette of a small room carved
in dry wood
or freshness of fountain and shadow
drowned in detail

Lifted faded fragments
scratch the surface

If you need detailed proof of my subordination draft the main
orthogonals of the construction

it's the same

roses violets and lilies
sage hyssop marjoram
or the part in the sun
aromatic

I know that the gardens
would have been made

marvelous

I begin again

Index

A:

abelias: 62, 74; abundance: 34; acaena: 45; acanthus: 62; accident: 31; accumulations: 34; actions: 65; actors: 28; adaptation: 84; addition: 14, 29; adventures: 106; aid: 79; air: 14, 39, 90; alcove: 7; alignment: 92; alignments: 34, 50; allure: 87; ambition: 24; angle: 19, 31, 39, 92; angles: 46, 81; animals: 7, 22, 23, 50, 107; answer: 65; anxiety: 107; anything: 33, 42, 86; apparitions: 50, 91; applause: 80, 105; approach: 51, 58, 82; approximation: 53; aqueducts: 17; arabesque: 39; architect: 65; armors: 23; arms: 42, 97; arrangement: 30, 43, 101; arrangements: 11, 74; art: 37; artifice: 81; asparagus: 43; aspect: 98; assaults: 106; assemblage: 8; assemblages: 37, 50; associations: 53; astonishment: 19; attachment: 40; attention: 21; attitudes: 23, 57; avenue: 7; avenues: 16; azaleas: 97.

B:

background: 35, 39, 50, 85; balance: 27, 53; balconies: 30; balcony: 8; band: 7; barrier: 22; barriers: 33; base: 43, 51; basis: 16, 47; bathers: 101; bathroom: 7; beasts: 91; bed: 25, 59; beech: 63; beginning: 105; begonias: 51, 91; behavior: 44; behaviors: 53, 97; bench: 8, 25, 49; benches: 40, 65; birdhouse: 7; birds: 32, 40; birth: 85; blackbirds: 107; blend: 65; bliss: 42; blocks: 82; bloom: 21; blue: 46; blueprint: 49; blues: 35, 73; boat: 8; boats: 16; bodies: 23, 57; book: 8; borders: 58; bouquet: 7 ; bouquets: 35, 39; box: 8; boxes: 20, 33; brakes: 103; branches: 26, 42; breeze: 19; breezes: 13; bridge: 7; bridges: 16, 22; brightness: 86; brow: 44; brushstroke: 69; bubblings: 47; builder: 17; buildings: 16, 36; burdens: 101; burrow: 20; bursts: 24; bush: 8; bushes: 70; butterflies: 40.

C:

calculations: 38; camouflage: 95; campfire: 8; canaries: 107; candles: 24; capacity: 35; carafe: 43; cardboard: 20; carousels: 16; castles: 63, 105; cats: 40; catuflorus: 11; cavern: 7; caves: 33; ceanothus: 11; cedar: 7 ; cements:

92; center: 52, 80; certainty: 92; cessation: 34; chains: 40; chair: 8; chairs: 23, 34; chance: 60; changes: 14, 18, 20, 53; chaos: 53; characteristic: 52; child: 107; chipboard: 91; chirping: 91; choice: 35, 48; choices: 68; cicadas: 26, 39, 91; circle: 30; circles: 46, 86; circulation: 34, 98; circumference: 35; circumstances: 60; classes: 101; clearing: 26; clearings: 13; cliché: 13; climbers: 32; clock: 7; clocks: 20, 82; closet: 8; closings: 48; clothesline: 7; clouds: 12, 35, 87; coat: 88; cold: 31; collapse: 40; collection: 8, 20, 22; collision: 59; colonnade: 7; color: 11, 19, 26, 43, 50, 52; colors: 23, 31, 37, 41, 43, 69, 104; column: 26; columns: 86; comforts: 79; commerce: 32; commitments: 60; complexity: 43; composition: 106; compost: 60; concentration: 87, 103; concern: 59; conclusion: 88; conclusions: 19; condition: 96; conditions: 33, 80, 89; confabulations: 67; confrontation: 95; confusion: 63, 65; conglomeration: 30; conjunction: 70; conks: 107; connections: 62; consciousness: 53; consequences: 28; consideration: 44; constraints: 99; construction: 39, 100, 108; contour: 11; contours: 41; contradictions: 97; contrasts: 69; conviction: 29, 44; coordination: 53; copies: 45; corner: 7, 19, 43; cotoneaster: 45; countryside: 22, 44, 58, 67; courtesy: 44; courtyard: 24; cover: 37; covers: 53; cradles: 37; craters: 46; creations: 33, 66, 67; crossouts: 25; crossing: 22; crossings: 25; crowd: 80; crumbling: 46; cube: 19; cubes: 87; cupid: 7; cure: 11; curiosity: 65; curious: 30; curtain: 31, 104, 105; curves: 43; cutlery drawer: 7; cuts: 7.

D:
dark: 34; dates: 50; day: 16; dazzles: 75; debris: 43; deceits: 101; decisions: 21, 27; decoration: 35; decorations: 24, 70; defaults: 25; definition: 50; delight: 39; demonstration: 101; density: 32, 84; depths: 21, 64; descents: 25; descriptions: 64; desk: 8; design: 23, 45, 63; designs: 30, 53, 63, 92, 101, 104; desire: 15, 46, 75; detail: 43, 108; details: 14, 70, 74, 103; detours: 8, 36; detritus: 91; development: 39; developments: 17; diagonal: 69; diagram: 43; difficulty: 15. 19, 99; diligence: 11; dimension: 67, 68, 94; dimensions: 21,

97; directions: 67; discomfort: 27; discovery: 14; discoveries: 49, 59; discretion: 11, 37; disorder: 26, 27, 34, 49, 93; display: 11, 52; dispositions: 25; dissemination: 27, 34; distance: 30, 59, 102; distraction: 30; distress: 30; ditches: 91; diversity: 64; divides: 82; dock: 85; dogs: 40; doors: 33; doubt: 14, 38, 75; dragonflies: 19; drape: 8; drawing: 13, 72; drawings: 36, 45, 61, 70, 87; dream: 105; dreams: 21, 50, 92; driftings: 30; droplets: 47; dynamics: 26.

E:
east: 23, 106; echoes: 41; eclipse: 59; edges: 48, 50; edging: 44; edifice: 93; effect: 22, 24, 32, 37, 38, 45, 53, 90; effects: 42, 47, 49, 58, 61, 64, 65, 70, 87, 90, 94; element: 38; elements: 16, 32, 67, 93; elephant: 24; elevation: 46, 82; elevations: 17; eloquence: 51; emulation: 38; enchantment: 48; enchantments: 98; enclosures: 84; encyclopedia: 64; end: 62, 65; enjambment: 63, 99; ensembles: 84; entryways: 16; epochs: 23; equilibrium: 82; erasure: 95; eternity: 39; event: 87; events: 28; everything: 15, 16, 67, 69, 83, 101; evidence: 74; evocation: 96; example: 17, 35, 38, 45, 70, 72; examples: 95; excess: 90; excitement: 43; execution: 103; exercise: 59; expanse: 97; expectations: 14; experience: 71; experiments: 69; exposition: 96; expression: 37, 39, 100; extension: 97; extent: 59; exterior: 16; eye: 18, 37, 81; eyes: 12, 72, 102.

F:
fabrics: 45; façade: 51; 58; face: 15; faces: 30; fact: 59; factor: 11; facts: 72; faith: 71; fall: 53; families: 28; fantasies: 92; fantasy: 11; 17; 63; farm: 24; fatigue: 29; fault: 71; faults: 40; fauna: 19; favor: 48; fear: 53; fears: 21; features: 13; fence: 51, 53; fences: 37, 75; field: 8, 27, 63, 64, 91; fields: 33, 36; figure: 24; figures: 30, 41, 43, 50, 67, 85, 103; figurines: 28; filth: 47; finches: 107; fire: 86; fish: 21, 47, 53; flashes: 67; flexibility: 88; flight: 7, 17, 80, 81; flights: 35, 74; floor: 22; flora: 11; flowers: 49, 64, 74; folds: 12; foliage: 23, 32, 45, 69; follies: 16, 17; follow-through: 61; foot: 18, 68; foot-

prints: 30; force: 38; forces: 106; foreground: 43, 74, 85; forest: 21; forests: 16; form: 24, 27, 31, 38, 46, 59, 63, 72, 74, 89; formation: 105; formations: 16, 106; forms: 14, 17, 29, 38; formula: 38; formulas: 99; fortunes: 67; fountain: 70, 80, 108; fountains: 8; fractions: 21; fragments: 108; frame: 12; frames: 30, 96, 101; freedom: 49; freshness: 108; friction: 38; friends: 30; frieze: 102; fruit: 11; fruits: 58; fun: 40; function: 17; furniture: 34, 98.

G:
gain: 24; gamble: 50; game: 38; garage: 7; garbage: 26; garden: 11, 17, 30, 41, 43, 53, 61, 64, 105; gardener: 65; gardening: 73; gardens: 17, 108; gargoyles: 80; garlands: 20; gates: 48; gaze: 102; geometries: 34; geometry: 30; geraniums: 51; gesture: 93; gilding: 35; 63; glue: 59; gnats: 104; gnomes: 13; goals: 23; grace: 24; graffiti: 36; granite: 83; grass: 48, 50, 58, 104, 106; gravel: 58; green: 26, 88, 97; greenery: 32; greenhouse: 8; greens: 48, 73; grid: 22, 24, 31, 69, 82; grids: 58, 101; ground: 92; groves: 70; guesswork: 93.

H:
habit: 13, 72; habits: 21, 24, 34, 38, 84; half-basin: 90; half-map: 41; half-world: 40, 89; happiness: 98; hand: 24; hands: 71; harmonies: 49; harmony: 11; hatchings: 65; havens: 39; heap: 11, 26; heat: 96; heater: 8; heating: 42; hedge: 8, 84; hedges: 49; hell: 26; help: 31, 64; herbariums: 104; hereda: 45; hesitation: 34, 96; highways: 16; hills: 70; hindrance: 41; hint: 21; historian: 65; hitch: 71; holly: 62, 63; hooks: 35; horizon: 15, 41; horizontals: 18; hour: 11, 36; huts: 17; hypothesis: 57, 66, 91; hyssop: 108.

I:
idea: 31, 53, 71, 89, 94, 95, 100, 105; ideal: 103; ideals: 67; ideas: 20, 35; illumination: 24; illusion: 12, 22; image: 11, 38, 62; images: 64; imitations: 67; immensity: 44; imminence: 45; impressions: 50, 82; impulse: 11, 38; inclination: 21; indifference: 51; inscriptions: 36; insects: 32, 40; insides:

28; installation: 51; instance: 99; instant: 14, 44, 70, 74; intentions: 28, 92; interest: 35, 42; interim: 39; interior: 16; interphenomena: 61; intervals: 49, 84; invention: 13; inventory: 105; inversions: 82; irrelevance: 21; irritation: 42; island: 25; islands: 106; isolation: 25, 84.

J:
joy: 34, 61; joys: 43; july: 62.

K:
kinds: 89; knots: 70; know-how: 100.

L:
lack: 39, 42, 100; lake: 8; lambs: 107; lamps: 20; land: 17; landmarks: 27, 37; landscape: 16; language: 26; laugh: 93, 105; lawn: 8, 70; lawns: 16; layout: 21, 30, 48, 87, 98; leaves: 86; legs: 97; length: 73; lessons: 23; level: 22, 93; liberty: 66; light: 12, 50; lighting: 24, 49, 86; lightness: 36; lights: 24, 50, 70; ligularias: 45; lilac: 21; lilies: 108; limit: 53, 58; limits: 59, 66, 73, 82; line: 19, 24, 26, 27, 39, 40, 53, 58, 81, 96; lines: 15, 18, 26, 32, 63, 68, 74, 82, 99; linnets: 107; lions: 107; list: 91; litter: 58; lizard: 94; locales: 105; look: 18, 22; love: 105; luminosity: 32.

M:
machinery: 64; machines: 38; magic: 33; man: 42; manner: 15, 95, 105; manners: 29; map: 11, 16, 31, 43, 53; maples: 15; maps: 17, 19, 36, 64, 91; margin: 58; marjoram: 108; mark: 57; marquees: 80; marshes: 19; marvels: 22; mass: 14, 58, 72; masses: 31, 106; mastery: 87; material: 19, 60, 89; materials: 33, 45, 51, 53, 92, 97; matter: 12, 28; meadow: 107; meaning: 27; means: 92; mediocrity: 92; meditation: 97; melancholy: 91; memory: 66, 85, 102; method: 38, 43, 45, 73, 82; methods: 39, 53; middle: 58; mimeticism: 53; miracle: 38; mistake: 71; mixing: 19; model: 21, 31, 37, 53,

71; models: 13, 33, 35, 41, 49, 60; moderation: 97; moment: 48, 51, 90, 98, 102, 105; moments: 27; momentum: 80, 82; monday: 38; monochrome: 35; monologue: 41; monospace: 16, 74; monsters: 107; moon: 72; mornings: 42, 51; mosquitoes: 19; moss: 32, 59; motif: 102; motifs: 43, 69; motion: 12, 21; mountains: 104; movement: 38, 49; movements: 41, 45, 58; mud: 19; 36; museum: 41.

N:

name: 104; names: 19, 64, 74; narrownesses: 36; nature: 32, 45, 47, 53, 57; natures: 41; necessity: 101; niche: 8; night: 38, 42, 81, 104; nightingales: 107; noise: 64; noises: 33; nose: 46; notations: 93; note: 39, 62; novice: 37; nuances: 23, 38; nudes: 41; number: 11, 18.

O:

oak: 19; oasis: 8; object: 20, 67; objectives: 72; objects: 13, 24, 26, 28, 43, 58, 66, 90; observation: 74, 87; observations: 18; observer: 25, 82, 99; obstacles: 7, 22; oceans: 16; oddities: 17; oil tank: 7; opinions: 17; opportunity: 69; opposite: 14; orange: 97; oranges: 21; orchard: 43; order: 16, 87, 103; organizations: 34; orthogonal: 106; orthogonals: 108; other: 65, 94, 97; others: 71, 85; outhouse: 7; outline: 31; outskirts: 8; ovations: 70.

P:

pace: 15, 46; pages: 22; pagodas: 17; paint: 45, 47; painter: 53, 67, 68; painters: 33; painting: 52; panel: 51, 58; panoramas: 21; paper: 45, 63; paradise: 106; park: 8; part: 86, 98, 108; parties: 33; partitions: 33, 49, 92; partridges: 107; parts: 31, 47; pass: 8, 40; passage: 91; passages: 18, 20, 48; pasture: 8; path: 7, 8, 17, 22, 40, 60, 102, 104; paths: 15, 49; pathway: 15; patience: 41, 59, 73; patina: 33; pattern: 13, 22, 63; patterns: 11, 40, 43, 58; perception: 61; perfection: 62; period: 91; perspective: 18, 67, 74, 90, 93; person: 97; photograph: 64, 69; photographs: 31, 96, 98; phrase: 87; phyllostacys:

45; pickets: 31; pieces: 84; piles: 20, 30, 40; pillars: 33; pine: 26; pines: 39; place: 13, 16, 43, 44, 48, 84, 85, 86, 104; places: 11, 18, 47; plains: 16; planes: 26; planks: 16, 30, 35, 85; plans: 16, 17; plantation: 34; plant-ings: 16; plants: 11, 23, 25, 35, 39, 51, 73; plastics: 35; playroom: 90; plea-sure: 15, 23; plot: 58; point: 15, 27, 31, 53, 87, 95, 106; points: 25, 27, 39, 82, 104; poles: 30; polychrome: 81; pond: 25; ponds: 16, 47; pools: 13; poplars: 7; population: 48; porch: 51; porticos: 93; pose: 69, 99; position: 12, 20, 45, 74, 99; possibilities: 28, 103; possibility: 101; postcards: 27; postures: 23; pot: 60; potential: 74; pots: 86; poultry: 43; power: 29, 45; practice: 73; prairies: 16, 24; praise: 11; precision: 60, 73; predators: 32; preference: 42; presentation: 45; preservation: 15; pressure: 25; primulas: 45; princes: 30; princesses: 30; principle: 74; principles: 67; problem: 22, 61; procedures: 53; profundity: 21, 101; progress: 15; project: 19, 43, 82, 84, 103; projection: 104; proliferation: 42; promontories: 14; proof: 108; proportion: 99; propor-tions: 41; puddle: 35; pursuits: 60; pyramids: 34.

Q:
qualities: 96; quality: 29; question: 21; questions: 29; quirks: 97.

R:
radar: 61; rake: 64; rain: 12; range: 17; re-plantings: 50; realizations: 12; reason: 15, 30, 59, 68; recollections: 28; rectangles: 58; reds: 21; ref-erences: 22; relation: 38; reliefs: 45; repetition: 14, 48, 49; repetitions: 42; reply: 14; reports: 82; representation: 20; reproduction: 58, 74; resem-blance: 94; resources: 98; rest: 15, 16, 92; result: 16, 100; retreat: 12; rho-dodendron: 45; rhythm: 49, 70; ribbons: 40; ridge: 19; ridgeline: 70; riots: 19; risk: 93; risks: 82; rivers: 16; rock: 8; rocks: 25, 33, 58, 83; role: 75; roof: 83; room: 7, 43, 48, 104, 108; roots: 61; rose: 42; roses: 25, 108; route: 81; routes: 98; row: 11, 26; rows: 65, 73, 86; ruins: 33, 40, 70, 101, 102; rule: 100; rules: 29; rumors: 14; rush: 40, 80.

S:

sand: 7, 32; sage: 108; saturation: 88; scale: 37, 49, 53, 70; scales: 41; scratches: 47; scene: 11, 30; scenery: 16, 46, 68; scenes: 45; scrapings: 26; scrawlings: 36; screens: 39; scribbles: 36; sculptures: 92; sea: 7; seas: 21; season: 64, 65; seasons: 21, 44, 74, 105; seat: 58, 63; secret: 51; section: 50; sedge: 45; seed: 106; seedlings: 101; sense: 14; sentiments: 11; sequence: 14; series: 33, 34; serrations: 27; setting: 24; shade: 50; shadow: 7, 96, 108; shadows: 42, 53, 57, 90; shape: 39; shapes: 16, 27, 37; sharpness: 81; shed: 7; sheds: 40; sheep: 22; sheets: 53; shell: 21; shelter: 98; shelters: 13; shield: 16; shoes: 43; shortcuts: 68, 90; shovel: 44; shrubs: 52; side: 34, 36, 46, 48, 58, 61, 85; sides: 38; sight: 12; silence: 42; silhouette: 108; silt: 15; simulacra: 67; singing: 107; sink: 8; site: 48; situation: 40, 90; size: 97; sketch: 96; sketches: 43; skies: 33, 46; sky: 44, 72, 83; slabs: 107; slate: 83; slippers: 52; slope: 21, 22; snow: 16, 32; solitude: 42; solution: 63, 84; something: 12, 33, 53, 68, 83, 94; son: 70, 87; song: 106; sound: 12, 33, 41, 46; sounds: 53; south: 11, 106; space: 11, 13, 18, 27, 30, 39, 40, 68, 71, 80, 84; spaces: 17; spade: 45, 64; sparkle: 53; sparklings: 12; specialists: 39; species: 101; specks: 37; specters: 37; speed: 29, 103; spirits: 11; spotlights: 32; sprinkler: 64; sprinklers: 65, 101; sprout: 60; square: 44, 72; squares: 18, 101; stacks: 74; staffs: 23; stages: 65; stain: 50; stains: 57, 61; stairs: 7; stands: 30; stars: 21, 70; state: 11, 67; states: 65; statue: 25; statues: 20; stature: 95; steps: 68; stones: 32; stories: 28; stream: 7; streams: 19; stretches: 21; strings: 39; strip: 23; stripes: 38; strokes: 50, 69; study: 50; stuff: 100; stumps: 74; style: 49; 61; styles: 66; subordination: 108; substitutions: 82; success: 50, 53, 60; suggestion: 45; summits: 19; sun: 12, 72, 107, 108; sunset: 85; support: 35, 79; surface: 17, 108; surfaces: 50, 95; surplus: 103; surprises: 75; suspicion: 63; swamp: 15; sweep: 53; swimmers: 57; synthesis: 66; system: 75, 82, 95; systems: 29, 72.

T:

tableau: 7, 41; tables: 34; tap: 8, 45; tapestries: 40; tar: 86; task: 17; taste: 84; temperature: 12, 39; temptation: 29; tension: 15; tent: 30; terms: 45; terrain: 16; 18; tests: 37; theater: 105; theory: 84; thickets: 19; thing: 14, 90, 94; things: 16, 38, 40, 48, 51, 83; thorns: 48; thought: 16, 71; threshold: 25, 52, 102; ties: 86; tiles: 83; time: 12, 19, 20, 21, 30, 33, 44, 51, 53, 65, 90, 96; times: 60; tints: 13; tomorrow: 38; tone: 88, 98; tones: 30; tools: 29, 64; touch: 63, 88, 103; touches: 38, 82; trace: 24; track: 14, 58; tractor: 64; trail: 8; trajectory: 80; transformations: 37; transitions: 38, 59; trash: 22; tratiacus: 15; treatment: 50; tree: 25; trees: 16, 24, 27, 40, 106; trellis: 84; trenches: 24; triangle: 83; tributary: 82; tricks: 24; turn: 32; twigs: 86; twilight: 21; twine: 39; twisting: 84; twitches: 101.

U:

undergrowth: 19; unity: 23, 35, 106; unknown: 88; use: 23, 26, 29, 48, 84; uses: 40; uselessness: 35.

V:

value: 18, 23; vanishing point: 21, 49, 67; variations: 60; variety: 11, 71, 97, 103; varnishes: 91; vases: 20; vegetation: 11, 50; vehicle: 16; versions: 48; verticals: 18; vices: 53; view: 8, 12, 14, 15, 21, 25, 31, 35, 44, 46, 87, 95; views: 14, 24, 41, 49, 60, 101; violets: 108; vines: 11; virtue: 23; virtues: 41, 92; vision: 42, 59, 88; visions: 46, 59, 99; visitor: 101; voice: 38; voices: 38, 64; volume: 22, 86.

W:

waits: 25; wake: 13; walks: 18, 42; wall: 28, 102; wallpaper: 74; walls: 16, 33, 35, 36; wanderers: 30, 36, 75; wanderings: 20, 24; waste: 98; water: 8, 47, 104; waterfalls: 33; waters: 84; waves: 104; way: 18, 50, 52, 69; ways: 14, 37, 53, 66, 79; weariness: 11; weight: 86; wheelbarrow: 44; whims: 13,

92; white: 19; whites: 43; whitewash: 37, 67, 68, 97; whole: 13, 14, 16, 18, 29, 61, 75, 88, 106; wind: 12, 106; window: 24; windows: 8, 52; winds: 25; wire: 35; wish: 60; witnesses: 30; woman: 42, 85; wood: 20, 52, 86, 108; words: 33; work: 17, 84; world: 16, 71; worry: 65.

Y:
years: 33; yellows: 73.

Z:
zone: 20; zoo: 32.

This is the fifteenth title in the La Presse series of contemporary French poetry in translation. The cover image is a page from the original P.O.L Éditeur edition with handwritten notes by the translator. The series is edited by Cole Swensen, and this book was designed by Erica Mena. The text is set in Iowan Old Style with titling in Futura.

The La Presse list:

1. *Theory of Prepositions*
by Claude Royet-Journoud
translated by Keith Waldrop

2. *Wolftrot*
by Marie Borel
translated by Sarah Riggs & Omar Berrada

3. *Heliotropes*
by Ryoko Sekiguchi
translated by Sarah O'Brien

4. *Exchanges on Light*
by Jacques Roubaud
translated by Eleni Sikelianos

5. *It*
by Dominique Fourcade
translated by Peter Consenstein

6. *Conditions of Light*
by Emmanuel Hocquard
translated by Jean-Jacques Poucel

7. *The Whole of Poetry is Preposition*
by Claude Royet-Journoud
translated by Keith Waldrop

www.lapressepoetry.com